Mary McLeod Bethune

A Photo-Illustrated Biography
by Margo McLoone

Reading Consultant:
Dr. Gail Lowe
Anacostia Museum

Bridgestone Books
an Imprint of Capstone Press

Fast Facts about Mary McLeod Bethune
- Mary McLeod Bethune was a teacher.
- She started her own school with $1.50.
- She used charred wood for pencils and crushed berries for ink.
- She was an adviser to President Franklin D. Roosevelt.

Bridgestone Books are published by Capstone Press • 818 North Willow Street, Mankato, Minnesota 56001
Copyright © 1997 by Capstone Press • All rights reserved • Printed in the United States of America

Library of Congress Cataloging-in-Publication Data
McLoone, Margo
    Mary McLeod Bethune/by Margo McLoone.
    p. cm.--(Read and discover photo-illustrated biographies)
    Includes bibliographical references (p. 24) and index.
    Summary: Follows the career of the black woman who spent her life educating and
working to earn basic human rights for her people.
    ISBN 1-56065-515-1
    1. Bethune, Mary McLeod, 1875-1955--Juvenile literature. 2. Teachers--United States--
Biography--Juvenile literature. 3. Afro-Americans--Biography. 4. Women--Biography.
    I. Title. II. Series.
E185.97.B34M39 1997
370'.92--dc21
[B]
                                96-39533
                                 CIP
                                  AC

Photo credits
Schomburg Center, cover, 6, 10, 14, 16
Bettmann Archive, 4, 8, 12, 18
FPG, 20

Table of Contents

A Leader in Education

Mary McLeod Bethune grew up in a poor family. Her family did not go to school. But Mary learned to read and write. She felt that all people should have an education. She became a teacher and a leader for African Americans.

Mary started a school for poor African-American girls. The school provided training for work. Years later, it became a college for women and men. It was called Bethune-Cookman College. The college was in Daytona, Florida.

Mary worked to improve education for all young people. She advised President Franklin D. Roosevelt about problems in education. She also spoke about rights for all people.

Mary (in hat) was present when President Harry S. Truman signed the bill for National Freedom Day.

Born into Freedom

Mary McLeod was born on July 10, 1875, in Mayesville, South Carolina. She was the 15th child of Patsy and Samuel McLeod. Her parents were slaves until 1865. A slave is a person who is owned by someone else. Mary was their first child to be born into freedom.

Mary was special from birth. Unlike other children, she was born with her eyes open. This made her parents hope that she would do great things.

Mary grew up on a farm called a homestead. Her mother cooked and cleaned for a white family. Her father farmed. The whole family helped in the fields. They planted cotton and grew vegetables.

Mary's parents hoped she would do great things. Here, she is speaking to thousands of people in Madison Square Garden.

Early Life

Mary tended the vegetable garden when she was very young. Later, she picked cotton in the fields. Working in the cotton fields was difficult and tiring. The McLeod family made up games while they worked. This made working easier.

One day, Mary went to work with her mother. She played with the family's young daughter. Mary spotted a book. She picked it up and looked at the letters and words.

The playmate told Mary not to touch the book. The playmate also told Mary that African Americans should not read. From that moment on, Mary knew she would learn to read.

With help from teachers, Mary learned to read. Then she taught many African-American students.

Student

Mary was picking cotton when a stranger came to visit. The stranger was a teacher. She was looking for African-American students. Mary wanted to learn to read. But her parents needed her to work in the fields. Finally, they agreed to let Mary go to school.

Every morning, Mary woke up early to go to school. She walked five miles (eight kilometers) to Miss Emma Wilson's School in Mayesville.

Mary learned reading, writing, and arithmetic. She helped her family and neighbors who could not read. She read the Bible to her grandmother. She read letters for her neighbors. She kept track of her father's cotton sales.

Mary was once helped by a teacher. So she became one to help others become educated and earn a degree.

Teacher

Mary finished school in one year. She returned to picking cotton in the fields. She wanted to learn more. But she did not have the money to attend another school.

Then Mary was selected to receive a scholarship. A scholarship is an award that pays for school. She attended Scotia Seminary in Concord, North Carolina.

Mary graduated from Scotia Seminary in July 1894. She continued her education at Moody Bible Institute in Chicago. After a year, Mary returned to Mayesville. She wanted to teach in the school where she started.

Mary graduated from Scotia Seminary and attended Moody Bible Institute. Then she started teaching.

Yours,
L. Bett

Marriage and Family

Mary taught at the Kindell Institute in Sumter, Georgia. There she met Albert Bethune. They both sang in the church choir. Albert taught Mary how to ride a bike. They spent a lot of time together. They were married in 1898.

Mary and Albert moved to Savannah, Georgia. Albert worked in a clothing store. Their son, Albert, was born in 1899.

Mary took a one-year break from teaching to take care of Albert. Soon she became restless. She wanted to teach again. Mary's husband was not interested in her teaching. Soon they separated. Their son stayed with Mary.

She took a teaching job in Palatka, Florida. A friend took care of her baby during school hours.

After Mary and her husband separated, she started teaching in Florida.

Dreamer

Throughout her life, Mary had powerful dreams. One dream was about many young people. They were wearing suits and dresses. They were waiting for someone to help them.

Mary decided to start a school. She and little Albert moved to Daytona, Florida. Many poor African-American families lived there. Some cooked and cleaned in wealthy homes. Some helped build the railroads.

Mary had $1.50 to start a school. She rented a small house. She found four young students. Mary opened her school in 1904. It was the Daytona Educational and Industrial School for Negro Girls. Negro is a word once used to describe African Americans. Mary's dream was becoming real.

Mary started her first school without supplies and $1.50.

School Founder

Mary opened her school with four students. She still needed supplies for the school. She searched the neighborhood. Mary found charred wood to use for pencils. She mashed berries for ink. She made beds out of large sacks stuffed with moss.

Mary needed money to teach more students. A man named Mr. White respected her goal. He gave her $250. Mary used the money to build a school. It was built on land that had once been a junk yard. It was called Faith Hall. This was the start of Bethune College in 1906.

In 1925, Bethune joined with Cookman, a nearby school for boys. Mary was president of Bethune-Cookman College.

Mary took students from Bethune-Cookman College to visit with President Roosevelt's mother.

Human Rights Leader

Mary was a great educator. She became a friend of First Lady Eleanor Roosevelt. A first lady is the wife of the President of the United States. The two women had the same concerns. They wanted all people to be treated equally.

Mary toured Europe in 1927. She was treated differently there than in the United States. People respected her for her success. Mary returned to the United States. She lived in Washington, D.C., and continued working for equal rights.

On May 18, 1955, Mary died of a heart attack. She was buried on the grounds of Bethune-Cookman College. Her grave marker reads *Mother.*

Mary discussed the development of a youth program with First Lady Eleanor Roosevelt.

Words from Mary McLeod Bethune

"Let us band together and work together as one big brotherhood, and give momentum to the great ball that is starting to roll for Negroes."

Minutes from Federal Council on Negro Affairs, August 7, 1936.

"I leave you love, I leave you hope. I leave you the challenge of developing confidence in one another. I leave you thirst for education. I leave you respect for the use of power. I leave you faith. I leave you racial dignity."

Quote from her last will and testament written before her death in 1955.

Important Dates in Mary McLeod Bethune's Life

1875—Born in Mayesville, South Carolina

1884—Enters Miss Emma Wilson's School

1887—Enters Scotia Seminary in Concord, North Carolina

1894—Enters Moody Bible Institute in Chicago, Illinois

1898—Marries Albert Bethune

1903—Moves to Daytona, Florida

1904—Opens Daytona Educational and Industrial School for Negro Girls

1906—Builds Faith Hall in Daytona, Florida

1911—Opens McLeod Hospital on school grounds

1925—Bethune College and Cookman College merge

1927—Tours Europe

1935—Receives NAACP's Spingarn Medal

1955—Dies in Daytona, Florida

Words to Know

first lady (FURST LAY-dee)—the wife of the President of the United States

negro (NEE-groh)—a word once used to describe an African American

scholarship (SKOL-ur-ship)—an award that pays for school

slave (SLAYV)—a person who is owned by someone else

Read More

Johnston, Johanna. *They Led the Way*. New York: Scholastic, 1973.
Meltzer, Milton. *Mary McLeod Bethune: Voice of Black Hope*. New York: Viking Kestrel, 1987.
Olive, Burt. *Mary McLeod Bethune*. Indianapolis, Ind.: Bobbs-Merril, 1970.
Radford, Ruby L. *Mary McLeod Bethune*. New York: G.P. Putnam's Sons, 1973.

Useful Addresses

Mary McLeod Bethune Museum
1318 Vermont Avenue NW
Washington, DC 20005

Mary McLeod Bethune Foundation
640 Dr. Mary McLeod Bethune Boulevard
Daytona, FL 32114

Internet Sites

Mary McLeod Bethune
http://tqd.advanced.org/2667/bethune.htm
Bethune Museum Archives
http://www.mcps.k12.md.us/curriculum/socialstd/FT/
Bethune_Museum.html

Index